JUN 0 9 2005

W9-AQV-625

J 599 .312 JAN
Jango-Cohen, Judith.
Armadillos /

PALM BEACH COUNTY
LIBRARY SYSTEM
3650 SUMMIT BLVD.
WEST PALM BEACH, FLORIDA 33406

ARMADILLOS

BY JUDITH JANGO-COHEN

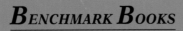

BENCHMARK BOOKS

MARSHALL CAVENDISH
NEW YORK

Dedicated to my brother Richard, who is fond of all creatures from the feathered to the scaly.

Series Consultant
James Doherty
General Curator, Bronx Zoo, New York

Benchmark Books
Marshall Cavendish
99 White Plains Road
Tarrytown, NY 10591-9001
www.marshallcavendish.com

Acknowledgments
The author wishes to thank the Burlington librarians for handling piles of inter-library
loans with a smile, and Molly Morrison, editor, for her insights and support.

Text copyright © 2004 by Judith Jango-Cohen
Diagrams copyright © 2004 by Marshall Cavendish Corporation

Maps by Ian Warpole

All rights reserved. No part of this book may be reproduced or utilized in any form or by any means electronic or mechanical including
photocopying, recording, or by any information storage and retrieval system, without permission from the copyright holders.

All Internet sites were available and accurate when sent to press.

Library of Congress Cataloging-in-Publication Data

Jango-Cohen, Judith.
Armadillos / by Judith Jango-Cohen.
p. cm. – (Animals, animals)
Summary: Describes the physical characteristics, behavior, and habitat of armadillos.
Includes bibliographical references and index.
ISBN 0-7614-1617-X
1. Armadillos–Juvenile literature. [1. Armadillos.] I. Title. II. Series.

QL737.E23J24 2003
599.3'12–dc21
2003003824

Photo Research by Anne Burns Images

Cover Photo by Animals Animals/Henry Ausloos

The photographs in this book are used with permission and through the courtesy of:
Corbis: Joe McDonald, 4; Visuals Unlimited: William Weber, 8 (top), 20, 42. Peter Arnold: Roland Seitre, 8 (bottom), 12; Gunter Ziesler, 16; Luiz
Marigo, 40–41. Photo Researchers: 9 (bottom). Roger Rageot/David Liebman: 9 (top), 25. Bruce Coleman Inc.: Jeff Foott, 14, 22, 26–27; Lee Rentz, 39. Animals
Animals: Michael Dick, 19; Stephen David Miller, 28; Fred Whitehead, 33; C.C. Lockwood, 34. World Images News Service: 36.

Printed in China

1 3 5 6 4 2

CONTENTS

1

INTRODUCING ARMADILLOS

A stringy-tailed, stubby-legged creature waddles along a Florida roadway. *Whoosh!* Cars whiz past and disappear–except for one. In this car, a young girl looks out of her window and calls, "Look! An armadillo!" Snatching her camera, and hopping from the car, the girl tiptoes toward the animal. She clicks one picture and then moves a bit closer. Too close! The armadillo dashes into a prickly patch of nettles.

The girl does not search for the armadillo in the nettles. If she did, the bristly stems would cut her. But the armadillo can hide in the nettles because a bony outer covering called a *carapace* protects its body. The top layer of the carapace is made of leathery scales. Buried beneath the scales are plates of bone. The carapace is hard, but it is not stiff like a turtle's shell. It is arranged into bands of bone connected by skin. These bands allow the armadillo to bend.

ARMADILLOS HAVE SCALY BACKS AND HAIRY BELLIES.

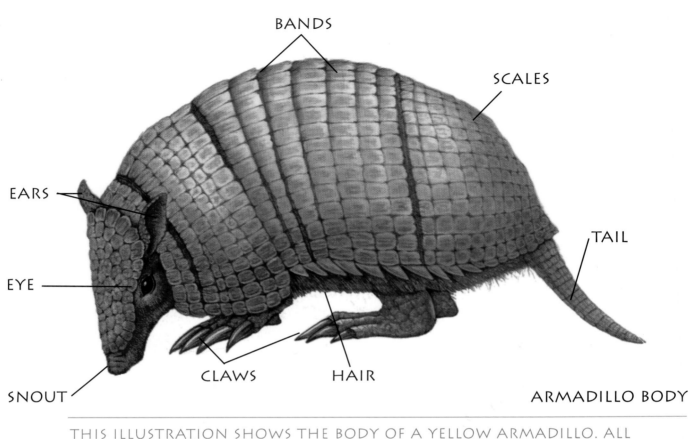

BANDS

SCALES

EARS

EYE

TAIL

CLAWS

HAIR

SNOUT

ARMADILLO BODY

THIS ILLUSTRATION SHOWS THE BODY OF A YELLOW ARMADILLO. ALL ARMADILLOS HAVE A BONY OUTER COVERING CALLED A CARAPACE.

Coated in armor, the armadillo looks different from other *mammals*. Most mammals have hairy or furry bodies. Their fur holds in body heat and shields them from the cold. The armadillo's carapace does not offer protection from freezing weather. This is one reason why armadillos live only in warm *habitats*.

Armadillos do not produce much body fat. Body fat

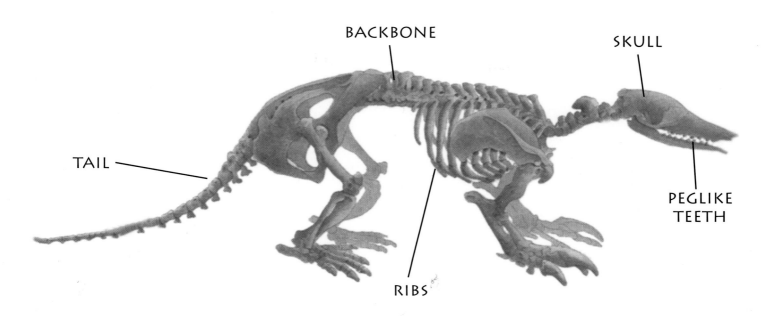

BACKBONE

SKULL

TAIL

PEGLIKE
TEETH

RIBS

ARMADILLO SKELETON

MOST ARMADILLOS HAVE VERY FEW TEETH. THEIR DIET OF INSECTS DOES NOT REQUIRE HEAVY CHEWING.

helps keep an animal warm. It also stores energy that animals can use when cold weather makes it difficult to find food. Since armadillos do not have a fat supply to rely on, they must eat year round. Winters must be mild so they can dig for insects, worms, spiders, lizards, and snakes. Sometimes they eat plant parts, such as shoots, fruits and roots.

ARMADILLO SPECIES

HERE ARE FOUR SPECIES OF ARMADILLOS WITH APPROXIMATE ADULT WEIGHTS AND LENGTHS:

NINE-BANDED ARMADILLO
17 POUNDS (7.7 KG)
31 INCHES (800 MM)

THREE-BANDED ARMADILLO
3.5 POUNDS (1.6 KG)
14 INCHES (350 MM)

GIANT ARMADILLO
110 POUNDS (50 KG)
5 FEET (1.5 M)

PINK FAIRY ARMADILLO
3 OUNCES (90 G)
6 INCHES (150 MM)

Because armadillos search the soil for food, they can only live in habitats that are suitable for digging. The ground must be soft enough to break up with their claws. It must also be free of snow or ice, which would make digging difficult. Lots of moisture is important too. Soft, moist earth is home to the crawling creatures that armadillos eat.

Armadillos find soft soil, food, and warm temperatures in the southern United States, Mexico, Central America, and South America. The most widespread of the twenty *species*, or kinds, of armadillos is the nine–banded. The only species in North America, the nine–banded armadillo also lives throughout Mexico, Central America, and much of South America.

Since nine–banded armadillos live in many places, they have had to adjust to different conditions. In Mexico, days are hot all year long, so they hunt during the cooler

RUDYARD KIPLING WROTE A STORY EXPLAINING THAT ARMADILLOS WERE CREATED FROM A TORTOISE AND A HEDGEHOG. THE AZTEC WORD FOR THE ARMADILLO IS "TURTLE-RABBIT." BUT SCIENTISTS HAVE FOUND THAT ARMADILLOS ARE NOT CLOSELY RELATED TO ANY OF THESE OTHER ANIMALS. THEIR CLOSEST RELATIVES ARE SLOTHS AND ANTEATERS OF CENTRAL AND SOUTH AMERICA.

NORTH AMERICA

ATLANTIC
OCEAN

CENTRAL
AMERICA

PACIFIC
OCEAN

SOUTH
AMERICA

NINE-BANDED
ARMADILLO

THIS MAP SHOWS WHERE NINE-BANDED ARMADILLOS LIVE. THEY CAN BE FOUND AS FAR NORTH AS KANSAS AND NEBRASKA.

evenings. In areas like Missouri, however, nights can get cold in winter. To avoid frosty temperatures, this armadillo changes its schedule and hunts during sunny winter days.

When not searching for food, the nine-banded armadillo rests in its *burrow*. Long, hooked, spiky claws scratch out a hole that is sometimes shared with rabbits, skunks, and possums.

The three-banded armadillo rarely digs its own burrow. It may use an old anteater hole or simply nap under a bush. To keep warm, the three-banded armadillo traps some body heat in pockets beneath its carapace. When attacked, it tucks its feet up into these spaces and rolls into a perfect little ball. In this position, its head and soft belly are not exposed.

The strangest looking species is the pink fairy armadillo. It resembles a furry slipper. Pink leathery bands line its back from nose to tail. Fluffy white hair fringes its sides. The pink fairy is only about 6 inches (15 cm) long, and weighs less than a stick of butter, about 3 ounces (90 g).

Giant armadillos, the largest species, are about the size of a large dog. Tiny termites are their favorite food. The giant armadillo hunts at night and often burrows

SIX-BANDED, OR YELLOW, ARMADILLOS HAVE BETWEEN SIX TO EIGHT BANDS
ON THEIR BACKS.

HAIRY ARMADILLOS OF SOUTH AMERICA AVOID THE SUMMER HEAT BY BECOMING MORE ACTIVE AT NIGHT. WHEN THINGS COOL OFF IN THE WINTER, THEY HUNT FOR FOOD DURING THE DAY.

near termite mounds so food is easily within reach.

All armadillos, from the giant to the fairy, are skillful diggers. They dig burrows to live in, holes to escape from *predators*, and each day they must dig for their dinner.

2

DIGGING UP DINNER

A quiet stream in Brazil glitters with spangles of light from a midnight moon. *Clump! Clump! Clomp!* Something is moving in a burrow by the bank. Out pokes a naked pink nose, tiny shining eyes, and a hunched armored back trailed by a scaly tail. A giant armadillo has woken up. Sloshing into the stream, it scares off a raccoon that is raiding a nest of bird eggs. After a few slurps of water, the armadillo tromps to the shore.

Despite the bright moon, the armadillo cannot see well. Unlike other animals that are active after dark, such as cats and crocodiles, armadillos do not have good night vision. Their eyesight during the day is also poor. The giant armadillo uses its sense of smell to find a meal. It plows along with its nose in the dirt, sniffling and snuffing for buried treats.

The giant armadillo's nose leads it to a towering mound in a grassy field. It looks like a stranded sand castle. With

THE MIDDLE CLAW ON A GIANT ARMADILLO'S FRONT FOOT IS LONGER THAN THE PINK FAIRY ARMADILLO'S ENTIRE BODY.

a snort, the armadillo raises itself onto its rear legs and muscular tail. Now as tall as the tower, the giant armadillo slices the mound open with swipes of its claws. Trickles of termites spill from the nest, and the armadillo digs into its breakfast.

With one flick of its tongue, the armadillo collects clumps of insects. The termites stick because an armadillo produces thick gooey *saliva* that coats its tongue. This sticky tongue is also strong. Armadillos use it to mash their food. Giant armadillos also have about one hundred back teeth for crushing food.

After savoring mouthfuls of termites, the giant armadillo moves on in search of a second course. Snorting and grunting, it smells something just below the surface. *Scritch! Scratch!* The giant armadillo digs into a patch of rotting leaves, uncovering a dead bird. A fly has laid her eggs on the bird. From these eggs are hatching young flies

GIANT ARMADILLOS CAN WEIGH AS MUCH AS A SMALL HUMAN ADULT. BUT THEY ARE PUNY COMPARED TO SOME OF THEIR SOUTH AMERICAN ANCESTORS. THESE *EXTINCT* GIANTS HAD ARMORED SHELLS THAT WERE 10 FEET (3 M) LONG. ANCIENT SOUTH AMERICANS USED THESE ENORMOUS SHELLS AS ROOFS FOR THEIR SHELTERS.

AN ARMADILLO'S LONG TONGUE CAN REACH INSECTS HIDING IN HOLES.

ARMADILLOS HAVE RINGS OF BONY SCALES PROTECTING THEIR TAILS.

called maggots. The giant laps up the white wiggly maggots. It also nibbles a bit on the decaying carcass.

Now the sky is beginning to lighten. But the armadillo wants dessert before heading into its burrow, so it shuffles into a cornfield. Raccoons have already been here, leaving nibbled corncobs behind. Ignoring the raccoons' left-overs, the giant armadillo sinks its claws into the loose, moist earth. Its strong front legs scoop out the dirt, which piles up beneath its belly. Then its rear legs kick the dirt out in a dusty spray. The giant armadillo has found its bedtime snack—juicy, squirming worms.

3
LITTLE PINK PUPS

One early evening in Mexico, a breeze whispers through the new spring leaves. Interrupting this drowsy sound is a busier noise coming from the base of a tree. A female nine–banded armadillo is clawing and scraping up grass and leaves. Gathering a clump with its front feet, the armadillo bounces backward on its rear feet. Guided by its tail, the armadillo backs into its burrow beneath a bush at the foot of the tree. In a chamber at the end of a tunnel, the armadillo drops its soft, leafy bundle. Then it scampers out to collect more material to line its nest.

The following day, the bustling little armadillo is not around. It is inside its burrow with four new pups. Last summer, this female armadillo mated. The male went off on its own, leaving the female to raise the pups.

The four pups are identical to one another, just as human identical twins are. This is because after mating,

A NEWBORN ARMADILLO SNIFFS ITS MOTHER'S SNOUT.

the mother armadillo has only one egg growing inside her. The egg makes a copy of itself and splits in two. Then each of these two eggs makes a copy of itself and divides. This produces four identical armadillos. Having identical babies is rare for humans, but not for nine-banded armadillos. They usually have a group of four identical pups called *quadruplets*.

Not all armadillos regularly give birth to four pups. The three-banded and giant species usually have only one. But seven-banded armadillos may have four, eight, or sometimes twelve pups per litter.

An armadillo pup looks like a little pink piglet with tiny eyes, stubby legs, and a pug nose. Its soft carapace is shiny and smooth like a snake's scaly skin. But gradually, bony plates will grow inside the skin and the carapace will stiffen.

A GROUP OF SCIENTISTS WAS SURPRISED WHEN AN ARMADILLO THEY WERE STUDYING GAVE BIRTH TO PUPS. WHAT WAS SO SURPRISING? THE ARMADILLO HAD BEEN CAPTURED TWO YEARS BEFORE, AND HAD NOT MATED SINCE. RESEARCHERS HAVE DISCOVERED THAT WHEN AN ARMADILLO IS UNDER STRESS, IT CAN DELAY THE DEVELOPMENT OF ITS EGG. THEN, WHEN CONDITIONS ARE RIGHT, THE EGG SETTLES DOWN TO GROW.

ARMADILLOS ARE BORN WITH A DESIRE TO DIG.

ARMADILLOS DIG LONG BURROWS
TO SLEEP IN, AND SHORT BURROWS
TO ESCAPE FROM PREDATORS.

THE NORMAL BODY TEMPERATURE OF A NINE-BANDED ARMADILLO MAY BE 16 DEGREES FAHRENHEIT (9 DEGREES CELSIUS) LOWER THAN THAT OF A HUMAN.

Nine–banded armadillo pups are born alert and strong. Their eyes are open, and during the first few hours they struggle to stand. Soon they stumble about the nest, crawling and tumbling over each other. The mother armadillo stays in her burrow more than before. She must be there to feed her pups. While she lies on her side, the four pups snuggle close to her and fill up on a meal of milk. They drink, nap, and play. The under–ground nest is their whole world for the first few weeks.

Then one cloudy day, the mother armadillo clambers out of her burrow beneath the tree. Behind her are four perky pups. There are many new smells for the pups to explore. They poke their snouts under rocks and leaves. Their mother rips into a rotting log and snaps up beetles. On these walks with their mother, the pups will learn to hunt. They will also learn to outwit predators.

4
ARMADILLO DEFENSES

A line of shiny–shelled turtles basks on a fallen tree limb in a Texas pond. On the sunny shore, a nine–banded armadillo lounges on its back. Its eyes are closed and a cool coat of mud covers its face and hairy belly. Suddenly, the armadillo rolls over and stands on its hind legs. Its sensitive snout sniffs to the right and then to the left. Dropping down on all fours, the armadillo scuttles into the water.

Out of the surrounding woods bounds a big–pawed puppy, followed by two boys. The wary armadillo has already sunk to the floor of the pond, and is plodding to the opposite shore. While it crosses under water, the armadillo does not have to come up to breathe. It can hold its breath for several minutes. When it finishes crossing the pond, the armadillo waits just below the water's surface.

WHEN THREATENED, THE THREE-BANDED ARMADILLO CAN TURN INTO A SMALL, SCALY BALL.

Meanwhile, the puppy is investigating the shoreline and has made its way to the far side of the pond. As the armadillo wanders out of the water, the puppy spots it. Lifting a curious paw, the puppy pats the armadillo's carapace. *Boink!* The startled armadillo springs straight up, sending the puppy tumbling backward.

When the armadillo lands, it scrambles over the sand, and furiously starts digging. Like a wound–up machine, the armadillo digs fast and deep. In the midst of this sandstorm, it does not get dirt up its nose. The armadillo holds its breath, as it does under water.

The puppy shakes itself off and continues watching, out of range of the sandy shower. The armadillo stops digging. Creeping over, the puppy sniffs at the protruding back and tail. Its little jaws gnaw on the bony armor, but are too small to get a grip. Just then, the boys catch up to their pet. One boy yanks on the armadillo's tail.

IF A BODY OF WATER IS TOO WIDE, AN ARMADILLO WILL NOT BE ABLE TO CROSS IT BY WALKING BELOW THE SURFACE. BUT THAT DOES NOT STOP THE ARMADILLO. GULPING MOUTHFULS OF AIR, IT INFLATES ITS STOMACH AND INTESTINES. THEN, WITH THIS BUILT-IN LIFE PRESERVER KEEPING IT AFLOAT, IT PADDLES TO THE SHORE.

ARMADILLOS ARE GOOD SWIMMERS AND OFTEN BUILD BURROWS IN STREAM BANKS.

AN ARMADILLO'S FIRST DEFENSE IS TO HIDE.

But the armadillo's carapace is wedged against the hole, and its claws are clamped into the dirt. Losing interest, the boys flip a stick into the pond, and the puppy plops in after it. Eventually the intruders move on. Then the nine-banded armadillo backs out of the hole and returns to its relaxing mud bath.

5
ARMADILLOS AND PEOPLE

One spring morning a girl skips out to water tomatoes in her Missouri garden. But instead of seeing a garden of neat rows, she discovers holes, heaps of soil, and several toppled tomato plants. Following the clues of dug–up dirt and tracks, the girl finds a burrow in the woods behind her house.

The next morning when the girl runs out to her yard again, she finds an armadillo. It is sitting unharmed in a wooden box that she put out the night before. A sliding door fell after the animal entered, trapping it inside. The girl releases the nighttime visitor, who waddles back to the woods. But the armadillo remembers the trap. It never again comes as far as the garden on its hungry search for bugs.

Nearby, a blueberry farmer is chasing armadillos. The animals jump up and run across the fields, trying to escape.

AN ARMADILLO SELDOM BITES, BUT IF YOU PICK ONE UP LOOK OUT FOR ITS LONG, SHARP CLAWS.

The farmer herds them into traps, taking them to a distant location to release them. Although they do not eat many blueberries, armadillos' industrious digging damages the plants' roots. But not all farmers are as patient as this one. Some shoot the armadillos that damage their fields.

People hunt armadillos for other reasons too. Throughout all areas where armadillos live, their meat is eaten. People in the United States sometimes call it Texas turkey. People also hunt armadillos for their carapaces. When dried, they are fashioned into baskets and handbags, with the tail for a handle. The carapace can also be made into a guitar–like musical instrument.

Some armadillos, like the three–banded, giant, and pink fairy, are *endangered.* This is because they are hunted by people, attacked by dogs, and their habitat is destroyed to make room for farms, homes, and highways.

Although they are hunted, armadillos are honored too. Some towns celebrate Armadillo Day. And in Florida and Texas armadillo races are held at county fairs. Images of armadillos are popular on belt buckles, T–shirts, jewelry, and toys. Texas even named the nine–banded armadillo as the state's official small mammal in 1995.

IN SOME AREAS, ARMADILLOS ARE CONSIDERED PESTS. WHILE HUNTING FOR FOOD, AN ARMADILLO CAN DO SERIOUS DAMAGE TO A CAREFULLY TENDED LAWN.

THIS THREE-BANDED SPECIES
LIVES ONLY IN BRAZIL, WHERE
DEVELOPMENT IS SHRINKING
ITS HABITAT.

OF THE TWENTY SPECIES OF ARMADILLO, ONLY THE NINE-BANDED CONTINUES TO INCREASE IN NUMBER.

The nine-banded armadillo is common in Texas today. But there were no armadillos there in 1845, when Texas became a state. Armadillos entered the region a few years later, coming up from Mexico. Today the nine-banded armadillo is found from Texas to Florida, and as far north as Nebraska. Its westward progress is hampered by dry conditions, since armadillos need at least 15 inches (38 cm) of rain per year. Cold winters keep it from moving farther northward.

Some armadillos have surprised scientists by moving into areas where it should be too cold for them to live. If the night air is biting cold, they come out to hunt when the sun can warm them. If there are not enough insects around, the armadillos make do with plant material, like berries. Armadillos are tough and flexible, like their bony-banded backs. Some researchers predict that armadillos may be able to live as far north as southern Massachusetts. Maybe one day in the future, a girl riding in a car through Cape Cod will call out, "Look! An armadillo!"

burrow: A hole dug by an animal to be used as a shelter or nest.

carapace: An animal's bony, outer protective covering.

endangered: An animal that is threatened with extinction.

extinct: When something no longer exists.

habitats: Places that have all the living and nonliving things that an animal needs to live and grow.

mammals: Warm–blooded animals that give birth to live young, and make milk to feed their young.

predators: Animals that hunt and eat other animals.

quadruplets: Four animals that are born together to the same mother.

saliva: The watery liquid in the mouth that moistens and partly digests food.

species: A particular kind of living thing.

BOOKS

Blassingame, Wyatt. *The Strange Armadillo.* New York: Dodd, Mead & Company, 1983.

Galvin, Laura Gates. *Armadillo at Riverside Road.* Norwalk, CT: Trudy Corporation, 1996.

Hopf, Alice L. *Biography of an Armadillo.* New York: G.P. Putnam, 1975.

Lavies, Bianca. *It's an Armadillo!* New York: E.P. Dutton, 1989.

Patton, Don. *Armadillos.* Chanhassen, MN: The Child's World, Inc., 1996.

Pembleton, Seliesa. *The Armadillo.* New York: Dillon Press, 1992.

Potts, Steve. *The Armadillo.* Mankato, MN: Capstone Press, 1998.

Squire, Ann O. *Anteaters, Sloths, and Armadillos.* New York: Franklin Watts, 1999.

Stuart, Dee. *The Astonishing Armadillo.* Minneapolis, MN: Carolrhoda Books, Inc., 1993.

MAGAZINES

Mealy, Nora Steiner. "Boinngg! Here Come the Armadillos." Ranger Rick, November 2000: 13–17.

Storrs, Eleanor E. "The Astonishing Armadillo." National Geographic, June 1982: 820–830.

WEBSITES

About Armadillos

www.armadillo-research.com/armadillo.html

Armadillo Central

www.everwonder.com/david/armadillo/index.html

DilloScape

www.dilloscape.com/index.htm

Window on the Woodlands: Nine-Banded Armadillo

www.flex.net/~lonestar/armadillo.htm

ABOUT THE AUTHOR

When Judith Jango–Cohen saw her first armadillo in Florida, she was not looking for it. She was in the car on her way to the Kennedy Space Center. Being from Massachusetts, she had never encountered the scaly mammal. It turned out to be just as fascinating as the rockets. Besides armadillos, Jango–Cohen has encountered lots of interesting creatures while traveling with her husband Eliot and her children Jennifer and Steven. You can find photos from their many trips at www.agpix.com/cohen.